# Easy Recipes 7

# Easy Recipes 7

## CHEF LILLE

**BookVenture Publishing LLC**
1000 Country Lane Ste 300
Ishpeming MI 49849
*www.bookventure.com*
Hotline:    1(877) 276-9751
Fax:        1(877) 864-1686


Ordering Information:
Quantity sales. Special discounts are available on quantity purchases by corporations, associ ations, and others. For details, contact the publisher at the address above.

Printed in the United States of America.

| Library of Congress Control Number | | 2018967031 |
| --- | --- | --- |
| ISBN-13: | Softcover | 978-1-64166-058-7 |
| | Hardcover | 978-1-64166-059-4 |
| | Pdf | 978-1-64166-060-0 |
| | ePub | 978-1-64166-061-7 |
| | Kindle | 978-1-64166-062-4 |

Rev. date: 09/21/2018

# Contents

I have created a recipe for the items that carry vitamin C, which is good for your gums!

Gengivitis is a disease that attacks most Americans!

Hope you will enjoy this book!

Vitamin C and antioxidants are found in oranges, lemons, strawberries, bok choy, yams, Brussel's sprouts... 75 mg daily is good for your cartilages, promoting the maintenance of collagen, the protein of the connective tissue; keeping the body protected against infections.

Ginger has a powerful combination of Vitamin C, Potassium and Magnesium, which, and, daily taken mixed with salt, makes your gum disease go away.

A cup of warm water mixed up with a coffee spoon of salt makes a very beneficial mouth wash!

The beauty in carrots is that they carry Vitamin C but also K, which is great for healing bleeding gums - chew on raw carrots!

Lemon has 58 mg of Vitamin C and I always add some to my steak and my drink.

Bok choy has 44 mg of Vitamin C in a cup; half a cup of orange juice carries the exact amount, 75 mg, and our minimum daily average; while half a cup of cooked Brussel's sprouts carries 48 mg of Vitamin C (we have a recipe for you).

I cup of yams carries 40 mg of Vitamin C (try our own Yams Medallions), and half a cup of strawberries carries 43 mg of Vitamin C, while a grapefruit has 72 mg of Vitamin C (you will have a party with our own Sangria and Rose Salads).

Baby Kisses

# Baby Kisses

## Ingredients:

1 can of condensed milk

1 cup of milk

1 stick of butter

1 bag of shredded unsweetened coconut

Little cup cakes

Cloves

## Method of Preparation:

Add the 2 spoons of butter in a pot, keeping the heat low. As it starts melting, add 2 cups of coconut and mix it with the milk.

Add 1 can of condensed milk and mix it well, until the dough comes off the bottom.

Turn off the fire and place the contents over a tray, spreading it out to cool.

On the side, prepare a bowl with coconut and create an assembly line as follows: Tray, coconut, little cake cups, serving tray.

Moisten your hands with butter and prepare a little oval shape; with your right hand pressure for the bottom standing the baby kisses on the palm of your left hand.

Roll them on coconut and place on the little cup cake, then on the tray.

As a final touch, place the clove on top.

Rose Salads

# Rose Salads

## Ingredients:

Lettuce

Grilled bananas

Grilled cheese

Potato chips

Flour tortillas

A French cup

Grapefruit

## Method of Preparation:

Wash a young head of lettuce and pull apart from the center leaves, cutting them into squares roughly with your hands, leaving out the center branches.

Wash the lettuce, yet again.

Turn on a grill.

Place on a grill a flour tortilla and butter both sides. Grill the tortillas, turning often, as soon as you see bubbles forming take it out and place into a French cup forming the rose.

Grill bananas sliced in half, and then grill mozzarella cheese.

Let them cool off.

Place in the bottom of the form the lettuce, on top cut the grilled bananas in little triangles, then slice the grilled cheese in triangles, as well, then top it off with potato chips.

Rose Salads

And how do we season our Rose Salads?

With Grapefruit Juice!

Sangria

# Sangria

## Ingredients:

Pinot Noir
Grapefruit
Don't dare throw sugar in it!!!

## Method of Preparation:

Cut the top of your Grapefruit and use that juice as a salsa for our salads.

Then, slice it alongside, and cut the slices in bits for the bowl.

Separate the seeds.

The taste of the grapefruit is so great that there is no need for additives, just let it soak in!

Add some more of the juice from the grapefruit, as you go, if the salad still lacks some moisture.

Pinot Noir only goes in the jar, though, for the Sangria.


Slice the grapefruit and add the Pinot Noir. We have a Sangria!

And it is a Party, with our Rose Salads seasoned with Grapefruit, the

same that is in the Sangria with Pinot Noir and Grapefruit. A Perfect Combination!

Who would say you could make a party of our salads?

It will be necessary, though, after you tasted your amazing salad and finished with the tender lettuce, sweet grilled bananas bathed in grape juice, and the roasted cheese; and you are left with the tortilla, to fill up your calyx with sangria, so you can dip your tortilla in it.

That's a pleasure in itself; all together this will be a wonderful experience with your senses..!

Oh, yes, we only have five of them…!

Yams Medallions

# Yams Medallions

## Ingredients:

1 package of tube yams

Nutmeg

Ginger root

Dry ginger

¼ tsp of ocean salt

2 cups of sugar

1 cup of water + water for boiling

## Method of Preparation:

In a small saucepan add 2 cups of sugar, 1 cup of water, ginger root

and start cooking on high heat. When you notice boiling has brought the sugar in a melting process, reduce the heat.

At the first sign of color, turn the heat off. The caramel will keep on cooking in the hot metal.

Boil the yams in a bigger pot, adding ocean salt and the ginger from the other pot, boiling all together for 15 minutes. Remove the skins and slice them in medallions, then place them in an oven form, sprinkling ginger and nutmeg on them. Pre-heat the oven at 350 degrees Fahrenheit.

Lay the caramel on top of the yams in the oven form. Pour ¼ cup of water in and mix.

Bake it at 350 degrees Fahrenheit for 8 minutes, raising it to 400 degrees Fahrenheit and baking it for another 2 minutes.

Remove the form from the oven by protecting your hands with gloves

and oven pad and by pulling the rack slowly and reaching for the form carefully, since it has melted caramel.

Brussels' Sprouts

# Brussels' Sprouts

## Ingredients:

3 branches of chives

3 regular potatoes

1 spoon of butter

2 cups of water

10 oz of Brussels' sprouts

1/2 teaspoon of garlic salt

½ teaspoon of onion salt

1 lemon herb branch

## Method of Preparation:

Place, in a pot, a cup of water, ½ teaspoon of garlic salt, 1 spoon of butter and 3 potatoes, (skinned, squared each into 6 parts).

Let it cook for fifteen minutes.

Add the Brussel's sprouts and ½ a teaspoon of onion salt. Cover the pot and let it cook for another ten minutes.

Add, then, the 3 branches of chives, sliced.

Mix it in, and bring it off the fire.

Place a branch of lemon herb on top.

Strawberry Jell-O

# Strawberry Jell-O

**Ingredients:**

1 pack of strawberries
2 packs of Strawberry Jell-O

**Method of Preparation:**

Place 1 cup of water to boil and prepare a form with strawberries, by washing them under running water and removing the pit.

On a glass bowl, place the contents of a package of Jell-O and add 1 cup of boiling water, mixing it together for a whole minute.

Pour on to the strawberries lined up in the form, carefully rearrange before putting it away overnight.

Prepare more strawberries for the bottom and prepare a second batch of Strawberry Jell-O, then place it in the refrigerator to cool for 2 hours.

Place a deep and bigger form with hot water, and use a knife to release the side off the mold of Jell-O.

Gently sit it in the hot water and place a plate on top, turning it around and placing it back in the refrigerator

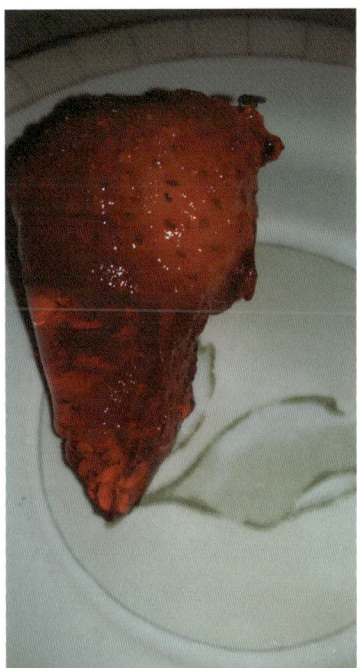

Sweet and Sour Chickpeas

# Sweet and Sour Chickpeas

## Ingredients:

16 oz. of chickpeas

1 branch of lemon herb

1 spoon of ground thyme

1 spoon of thyme leaves

1 spoon of minced garlic

1 spoon of garlic salt

2 lemons

2 spoons of grounded ginger

1 spoon of grounded paprika

1 teaspoon of cumin

¼ teaspoon of red pepper

2 spoons of butter

6 chives

1 spoon of parsley leaves

## Method of Preparation:

Place the chickpeas in a pot and cover with water. Bring it to a boil and turn off the fire. Let it sit for an hour.

Chop the chives and throw in the cooking pot, together with the ginger, minced garlic, onion salt, the juice of a lemon, both the grounded thyme and the thyme leaves, paprika and cumin, red pepper and the spoon of butter. Mix it and bring it to a boil.

After thirty minutes, add the juice of another lemon and let it sit, covered.

Add the perforated pot, together with a bottom pot and a lid.

And pour the contents through, using eye protection!

Add a second spoon of butter on the top of the chickpeas, spreading it around. Close the lid and turn on a medium fire.

In about **30** minutes a sauce will form, turn off the heat and dismantle the pots. The bottom part has the sweet and sour sauce that needs to be mixed.

Set the chickpeas with the sauce and a lemon herb branch.

Melon Centerpiece

# Melon Centerpiece

**Ingredients:**

1 small melon
Carving knife

**Method of Preparation:**

Draw a circle in the center, remove it, and then start carving petals around it, marking the opposite side, and dividing in two each of the resting portions.

In the center of the petal cut a triangular shape and pull it out.

Cut alongside the top of the petals, and start carving from the tip of a petal another petal that will end on the tip of the following petal, and slice from in between the new petals the outstand portion. As you finish covering the whole melon with petals, you will end at the other side, where you will carve, yet again, a circle, for the melon to be able to stand on itself.

Veggie Burger

# Veggie Burger

## Ingredients:

1 portobello mushroom

1 round bread

4 basil leaves

Bok Choy

Red bell pepper

Zuchinni

Olive oil

Onion salt

Paprika

Cumin

Balsamic vinegar

## Method of Preparation

Slice the bread not all the way through, but dead in the center, and then put it aside.

On a grill, add a thread of olive oil, onion salt, a dash of paprika and cumin to a minimum.

Turn it to medium heat and proceed to roast the bell pepers, cut in strips (slice a bell pepper in 4 strips, take away the crown and the seeds.)

Add onion salt and paprika to the top of the bell pepper.

Proceed to slice the zuchinni diagonally, and place them around the tray, also adding a dash of onion salt, cumin and paprika.

Add, now, the bok choy..

The last item to be added is the portobello mushroom, which is covered in olive oil, a bit of balsamic vinegar, onion salt, paprika and a bit of cumin, then turned around.

Move the elements in the tray, surrounding the mushroom with the roasted bell pepper, and turn the zucchini and bok choy over.

Set the zuchinni on raw bread; then the bok choy, and then the bell pepper. The portobello goes on top, next; followed by the basil leaves. Add, then, red bell pepper,

bok choy, zuchinni, topping it with red bell pepper. Close your sandwich.

STRAWBERRY SWEETENED CHEESECAKE

# Strawberry Sweetened Cheesecake

## Ingredients:

1 box of strawberries

4 eggs

1/3 spoon of flour

16 packages of sweetener

2 packages of 6 oz regular cream cheese

4 oz strawberry cream cheese

10 spoons of butter

4 oz condensed milk

## Method of Preparation:

Break the 4 eggs in a bowl and beat them together with the sweetener; add slowly the melted butter and the flour, bringing them all together.

Add the 2 regular packages of 6 oz of cream cheese and 4 oz of strawberry cream cheese, and then finally add 4 oz of condensed milk.

Pre-heat the oven at 400 F, and cover the form with parchment paper.

38 minutes of baking will take it to a perfect baking; then turn off the heat and open slightly the oven door, letting go off the steam.

After ten minutes remove the form carefully, wearing gloves and a pad, for holding it. Pull off the rack, at first; then, wearing also goggles for your eye protection, bend in with gloves and pad to pick up the hot form, being aware of your arms touching the oven's hot side walls.

Place it on a wooden table and let it cool off another twenty minutes.

Turn it upside down on a plate, and place it in the refrigerator. Now you wash the strawberries, 3 times, and then place them in cold water to finish taking the chemical insecticides away.

As 30 minutes goes by, slowly peel the parchment paper off the strawberry cheesecake.

Place the strawberries around the top of the cheesecake.

Refrigerate overnight.

Pork Loin

# Pork Loin

## Ingredients:

½ spoon of garlic salt

½ spoon of onion salt

½ spoon of paprika

½ spoon of cumin

1 cup of water

1 cup of Pinot Noir Wine

4 pounds of pork loin boneless

1 cup of mushroom tomato sauce

1 orange

Wooden sticks

## Method of Preparation:

Set the oven for baking at 350 degrees Fahrenheit. Place the loin in the center of an oven form, add 1 spoon of the dry mix and half a cup of wine.

After one hour, turn the loin around and add the other half of the Pinot wine, and 1 spoon of the dry mix.

Cover the form with Aluminum foil.

At 1:30 minutes add half a cup of mushroom tomato sauce, keeping the form covered.

At 2 hours, turn the loin around and add the other half of the mushroom tomato sauce, keeping the form covered set it in the center of the top rack.

At 3 hours, turn the loin over, to ensure even baking.

Slice the orange in 10 slices.

At 3:15, add the orange slices:

Add the orange slices firmly, by pinning them to the top first.

Turn the pork loin upside-down and pin the orange slices firmly by applying wooden sticks.

Count those wooden sticks, because at the very end they need to be pulled out.

Prepped:

At 3:30, turn the loin over, and reposition the slices, if needed, by pulling off the existent wooden sticks, and placing them back pinning the orange slices into place.

Pull the aluminum foil out and add a cup of water to the broth.

At 4 hours raise the oven temperature to 150 degrees Fahrenheit and turn the loin over, repositioning the sticks by grabbing the orange back.

At 4:15, turn the loin over again, to ensure even roasting, always repositioning the orange slices, even at the sides.

At 4 hours and thirty minutes change the settings to broil at High and turn the loin over, making sure to pull out the sticks on site and letting the orange slices incorporate into the broth.

At 4 hours and forty-five minutes turn the loin over for the last fifteen minutes, pulling out all the sticks left off the orange slices and letting them incorporate into the broth, as long as they don't have wooden sticks glued to them.

Clear off all of the wooden sticks.

Strawberry Yogurt

# Strawberry Yogurt

**Ingredients:**

1 strawberry yogurt
½ a package of strawberries
1 spoon of flour
1 pack of cream cheese
3 spoons of butter
1 egg
10 packages of sweetener

**Method of Preparation:**

Wash the strawberries and remove the grimaces, pit and hard parts (as well as too softened ones). Once the strawberries are cleaned, quarter them and set some triangular shaped slices apart.

In a bowl, beat the cream cheese, butter and spoon of flour, together with the 10 packs of sweetener. Add the strawberries by spoon, mixing them in. Add the yogurt, at last.

**Lemon – Strawberry Yogurts**

# Lemon - Strawberry Yogurts

**Ingredients:**

1 strawberry yogurt

½ a package of strawberries

1 spoon of flour

1 lemon

1 pack of cream cheese

3 spoons of butter

1 egg

10 packages of sweetener

**Method of Preparation:**

Wash the strawberries and remove the grimaces, pit and hard parts (as well as too softened ones). Once the strawberries are cleaned, quarter them and set some triangular shaped slices apart.

In a bowl, beat the cream cheese, butter and spoon of flour, together with the 10 packs of sweetener. Add the strawberries by spoon, mixing them in. Add the yogurt.

Juice the lemon and mix the juice in.

Keep them safe!

Orange Smoothie

# Orange Smoothie

**Ingredients:**

3 oranges

2 peaches

1 pear

2 cups of water

6 sweeteners

**Method of Preparation:**

Place in a blender the juice of 3 oranges; then add 2 peaches cut in quarters and off their seed, taking off both extremities; the same with the pear: cut around the seed and cut away from both extremities.

Add 2 cups of water and the contents of 6 sweeteners.

Beat for 2 minutes, or until you feel the blender running smoothly.

Plum Juice

# Plum Juice

## Ingredients:

2 oranges

10 strawberries

2 plums

2 packs of sweetener

½ cup of water

## Method of Preparation:

As seen in the picture, skin and slice in squares 2 oranges, then add 10 strawberries, pitted and washed, then sliced; at last add the plums, washed and quartered.

Add the 2 packs of sweetener and ½ a cup of water, then mix for 2 minutes.

Vegetarian Fettuccini

# Vegetarian Fettuccini

## Ingredients:

Pitted green olives

1 green bell pepper

1 yellow bell pepper

1 red bell pepper

1 onion

3 teeth of garlic

1 pack of sliced mushrooms

1 pack of baby mushrooms (whole)

Whole wheat fettuccini

Paprika

Cumin

Dill

Rosemary

Ocean salt

2 spoons of butter

Olive oil

## Method of Preparation:

Take 3 teeth of garlic, skin them, take the dry top off, square them and throw them in melted butter, cover them with sprinkles of ocean salt and turn the fire on low.

As the butter starts to burn, add 1 spoon of olive oil.

Pitt the bell peppers, remove the seeds, and julienne them off.

Roast the green bell peppers and use a thread of oil on top of the bell peppers, adding the ocean salt. Cover with a lid, turn them around in 2 minutes, add some salt, paprika and cumin, Top it off with the mushrooms, add dill, put on the lid and time it for 3 minutes.

Julienne the onion on top of it. Mix and add 1 spoon of butter and more olive oil, mix it, turn it over, and add rosemary on top.

Cover and let it boil for 2 minutes. Do not go over 5 minutes with the bell peppers. Turn the fire off.

On a big pot, add 1 spoon of ocean salt and 1 spoon of butter, bring it to a boil and lay in the fettuccini, timing it for 8 minutes.

When the buzz goes off, dry the fettuccini and add to the sauce previously prepared, mix it, tussle and add 1 spoon of butter. Top it off with the pitted olives, mixing it together.

It's delicious!

Pineapple Pork Shoulder

# Pineapple Pork Shoulder

**Ingredients:**

1 can of pineapple slices in light syrup

A whole pineapple

2 ½ pounds of a whole pork shoulder

Garlic salt to taste

1 spoon of paprika

½ spoon of cumin

Honey

Seeded rye bread

**Method of Preparation:**

Mix together one spoon of garlic salt for each pound of the meat; the spoon of paprika and ½ a spoon of cumin.

Place the pork shoulder in the baking pot and spread it on top, turning it around and getting all of the seasoning in it.

Slice open the pineapple, take off the top and sit it on it, cutting longitudinally and making sure no dark spots are left behind. Remove the center, as well. Place it on the meat, with sticks. The set up goes as follows: the raw pinneaple goes underneath and the seasoned one goes on top. Make sure you get the tops and the sides, as well.

(Bake any meat for **90** minutes and add one hour for every extra pound of it.)

It goes in the oven as so, at **350** degrees Fahrenheit, for **75** minutes, because we are dealing with **2** pounds of meat.

After the timer goes off, we add honey threads on top, and then we place it back in the oven very carefully, using oven gloves and pulling the rack first, so we don't burn the arms in the oven. Raise the baking temperature to **450**, for **15** minutes. Cover it with a lid and bake for another **55** minutes, at **400** degrees Farenheit.

Uncover and raise the heat factor to **450** degrees Fahrenheit. Roast for **5** minutes more. Turn off the heat. Let it seat for ten minutes in the oven. Remove it from the oven, wearing oven gloves and being aware of your arms. Place it on a wooden table.

Take 2 slices off the rye bread, 1 of the pork shoulder and get one pineapple roasted slice to make your sandwich. Salt to taste.

Set it up again, and sprinkle paprika and garlic salt on the meat, covering it with new slices of pinneaple. Turn the oven to 250 degrees Fahrenheit, for 30 minutes, then raise it to 450 degrees Fahrenheit for 15 minutes, spreading honey on.

Raise it to 450 degrees Fahrenheit for another 15 minutes, and turn the heat off.

Wearing goggles and oven gloves, pull the rack off and pick up the dish with both hands, placing it on a wooden table. Slice the meat in ham fashion, and serve it with the roasted pinneaples.

Orange Lollipops

# Orange Lollipops

**Ingredients:**

6 Valencia oranges

¼ cup of water

2 sweeteners

Lollipop Tool

Blender

**Method of Preparation:**

Peel off the oranges, leaving the white skin on. Take off the tops and throw them in the blender with ¼ cup of water and 2 packs of sweetener.

Mix for 2 minutes, keep on the mixing, and finish mixing them for 3 more minutes.

Place the mesh in the lollipop containers, and set them in the freezer for 3 hours straight, or overnight.

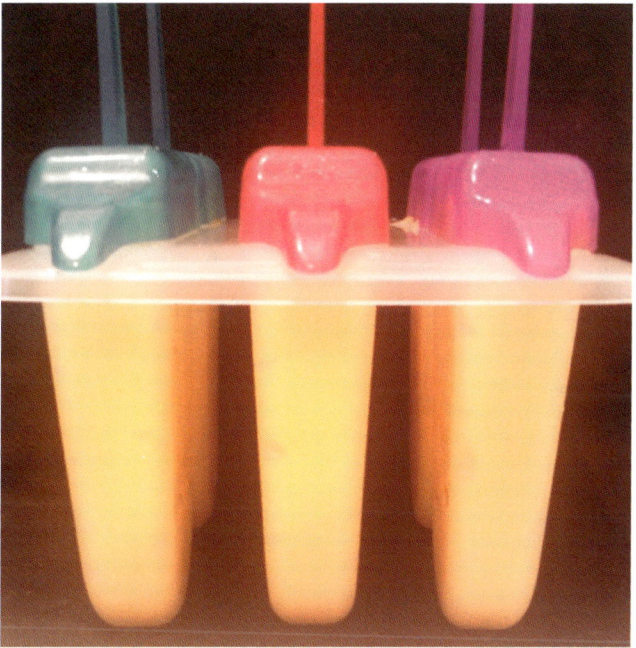

The morning after, prepare to lick your own sugar-free lollipop. That will taste awesome!

Pheasant with Sweet Potato Fries

# Pheasant with Sweet Potato Fries

## Ingredients:

1 pheasant

Olive oil

Thyme in powder

Ocean salt

Black pepper

2 oranges

2 apples

Cubed chicken

1 pack of frozen sweet potato fries

## Method of Preparation:

Remove the giblets and smear the powdered thyme inside and outside the bird, in between legs and wings, as well.

Salt the bird the same way.

Place it in an oven form and insert an orange inside the bird's body; place an apple at the head opening and another apple at the bottom.

Slice the second orange in 4, place a quarter in between the wings and by the legs, sustaining the bird; do the same at the other side.

Place in an oven and turn it at 250 degrees Fahrenheit.

On a separate pot, dissolve the chicken cube in a cup of water and add it to the pheasant.

At 5 minutes, spread olive oil on it, ocean salt and thyme.

At 10 minutes, lay on some Olive Oil, salt and thyme. At 15 minutes turn it over, and season with thyme and salt.

At 30 minutes season again, this time around using olive oil, thyme and salt.

At 45 minutes we apply the third seasoning, with olive oil, salt and thyme.

We have sprinkled 3 times on each side, now we wait for the 60 minutes to turn it over and cover with aluminum paper, so we must prepare the aluminum.

This is how it looks at 60 minutes, after we turn it over again.

Wrap it in aluminum paper and let it bake for another hour, at 250 degrees Fahrenheit.

At 100 minutes, we add sweet potato fries.

At 115 minutes we sprinkle black pepper and ocean salt on the sweet potatoes.

When the timer beeps, get the bird out and remove the fruits, discarding them. Place the clean pheasant in a dish, and the sweet potatoes aside.

You must remove the pieces of orange from the wings and thighs, the orange inside, and both apples, and discard them.

At 120 our sophisticated dish is ready, the sweet potatoes have acquired the flavors of the olive oil and seasonings, and our pheasant is cooked inside and out and ready to be digested with your favorite white wine.

Chef Lille wishes you the best of everything that your heart desires!

Enjoy it!

CPSIA information can be obtained at www.ICGtesting.com
Printed in the USA
BVIW120843280319
543964BV00009B/80